SEAMING & INNOVATION

A BASIC IDEA ABOUT SEWING MACHINE AND SEWING TECHNIQUES

FIONA PAULSON. T

• • •

This book is dedicated to all the Fresh minds who show interest towards Fashion and eager to learn more about the feild from basic to demandfull

• • •

Contents

Foreword

• • •

My whole carrier has been dedicated to pursue the vision of Fashion. I decided I wanted to give the textile sewing world the idea about fashion and how sewing becomes a major part in the Industry. The Basic Sewing technology comes with a mission to open, inform and connect the global fashion industry with the new innovation and technology. Fashion students being young budding enthusiastics need a basic idea about fashion and learn the art of sewing as the base knowledge for creating beautiful wonders in their future.

• • •

Preface

• • •

Its been long I have been coming to the idea to expose my mind with the budding fashion minds, giving them information about the basic idea and evolve themselves with the art of fashion and fabrics.

Basic Sewing dealing with styles, machines, art, manufacturing and learning about new innovations. The book primarilly makes the younf minds learn more about the sewing technology and processes while creating new innovative designs, to market around the world. This book is a stratergic and student oriented book to develop the innovative skills and creative thinking within oneself.

• • •

Acknowledgements

• • •

Writing this book has been more fullfilling than any other thought, rewarding than I ever imagined.

This would not have been possile without the support of my Mother and my better half, who constantly stood as my support system throughout my writing.

I, am eternal glad to my Institution and my fellow friends who encouraged me during my writing, staffs in Department of costume Design and Fashion for their help and support to carry out the work.

I, would like the thank our Almighty God for its supreme power without which this work would not have been a complete success.

• • •

Prologue

• • •

Congratulations!, the fact that youre reading this means you have taken one step closer to know more about Fashion and its basics to develop the idea design through the art of Sewing. Let this book gain you more knwledge about Fashion sewing machines and new innovations in the Fashion Industry.

• • •

CHAPTER I

Invension and History of Sewing Machine

HISTORY OF SEWING MACHINE

Charles Fredrick Wiesenthal, a German-born engineer working in England, was awarded the first British patent for a mechanical device to aid the art of sewing, in 1755. His invention consisted of a double pointed needle with an eye at one end.

Newton Wilson's copy of Saint's sewing machine.

Thomas Saint's chain stitch used on the first ever complete sewing machine design for leather work. An awl preceded the eye pointed needle to make a hole in preparation for the thread.

Animation of a modern sewing machine as it stitches

In 1790, the English inventor Thomas Saint invented the first sewing machine design. His machine was meant to be used on leather and canvas material. It is likely that Saint had a working model but there is no evidence of one; he was a skilled cabinet maker and his device included many practically functional features: an overhanging arm, a feed mechanism (adequate for short lengths of leather), a vertical needle bar, and a looper. Saint created the machine to overall reduce the amount of hand-stitching on garments, making sewing more reliable and functional. His sewing machine used the chain stitch method, in which the machine uses a single thread to make simple stitches in the fabric. A stitching awl would pierce the material and a forked point rod would carry the thread through the hole where it would be hooked underneath and moved to the next stitching place, where the cycle would be repeated, locking the stitch.Saint's machine was designed to aid the manufacture of various leather goods, including saddles and bridles, but it was also capable of working with canvas, and was used for sewing ship sails. Although his machine was very advanced for the era, the concept would need steady improvement over the coming decades before it could become a practical proposition. In 1874, a sewing machine manufacturer, William Newton Wilson, found Saint's drawings in the UK Patent Office, made adjustments to the looper, and built a working machine, currently owned by the Science Museum in London.

In 1804, a sewing machine was built by the Englishmen Thomas Stone and James Henderson, and a machine for embroidering was constructed by John Duncan in Scotland. An Austrian tailor, Josef Madersperger, began developing his first sewing machine in 1807 and presented his first working machine in 1814. Having received financial support from his government, the Austrian tailor worked on the development of his machine until 1839, when he built a machine imitating the weaving process using the chain stitch

SEWING

Before the invention of a useable machine for sewing, everything was sewn by hands. Most early attempts try to replicate this hand sewing method and were generally a failure. Some looked to embroidery, where the needle was used to produce decorative, not joining stitches. This needle was altered to create a fine steel hook – called an Abuja in Spain. This was called a crochet in France and could be used to create a form of chain stitch.

The ultimate look of the garment depends on how the patterned parts are attached together by means of sewing. Any variation in sewing will lead to defective material. Sewing is a tough as making pattern for any difficult style. Hence much concentration is to be paid while doing this job. Sewing can be classified into two groups and they are

- Hand sewing
- Machine sewing

Hand sewing can be best suited for some special and temporary purposes, it is not being dealt here, as most of the garments are machine made and mass produced. Our main emphasize is focused on to the machine sewing.

Generally machine sewing is carried out on materials like woven and knitted fabrics, particularly in textile applications. Again this may be on various fabrics having different quality parameters.

Different Parts of Sewing Machine:

- Spool pin,

- Bobbin binder spindle,
- Bobbin winder stopper,
- Stitch width dial,
- Pattern selector dial,
- Handwheel,
- Stitch length dial,
- Reverse stitch lever,
- Power stitch,
- Bobbin winder thread guide,
- Thread tension dial,
- Thread take-up lever,
- Needle clamp screw,
- Presser's foot,
- Bobbin cover,
- Bobbin cover release button,
- Feed dog,
- Needle,
- Needle plate

Basic Sewing Machine

TYPES OF SEWING MACHINE BED

Stitch type

- Flat bed sewing machine (basic)
- Lock stitch, chine stitch
- Raised bed machine
- Lock stitch, chine stitch
- Post bed machine
- Lock stitch, chine stitch
- Cylinder bed machine
- Lock stitch, chine stitch
- Side bed machine
- Chine stitch, over edge stitches.

SINGLE NEDDLE SEWING MACHINE

A machine for sewing leather, etc. specifically, one that uses two threads (an upper and a lower, or bobbin thread) and at sewing woven materials.

Terms used to describe parts of the sewing machine

- **Head**- The complete sewing machine without cabinet or carry case.
- **Bed**- The flat surface of the sewing machine. A flat bed machine has one level to sew on. A free-arm bed has a removable U-shaped part of the bed to reveal an arm or tub used for sewing hard-to-reach areas like pant cuff or sleeve.
- **Hand wheel**- The wheel located on the right side of the sewing machine. This wheel is driven by the motor, but may be turned by hand to adjust needle height.
- **Bobbin winder**- Mechanism used to wind bobbins.

- **Bobbin**- Low spool that provide the lower thread.
- **Thread take-up** – Arm that pulls up slack in thread.
- **Thread guide**- Device which carries thread to a certain location.
- **Upper tension** – Mechanism which control delivery of upper thread.
- **Lower tension**- Provided by the bobbin case. Controls delivery of the bottomed thread.
- **Bobbin case** – Device which holds the bobbin and provides tension to the lower thread.
- **Pressure Foot** – Foot that presses down on fabric to stabilize its movement.
- **Feed Dog** – Mechanisms which controls motion of the fabric.
- **Needle Plate** – Plate under presser foots with slots to allow feed dog to reach fabric and opening for the needle to move up and down.
- **Hook** – Device which picks the thread off of the needle.
- **Feed drop** – Adjustment used to take the feed dog out of play for free hand work.
- **Stitch length** – Adjustment used to determine length from back of the stitch.

HOW IT WORKS

The FIG shows the needle has its eye at the sharp end. The other end is attached to a rod that goes up and down inside fixed arm. The arm also holds a presser foot, which can be raised or lowered manually, but which kept down when sewing. Its role is to press the fabric against a base plate. The needle plunges in to the fabric from the top, through a thread tensioning mechanism, and through the eye of the needle.

This is another thread, which comes up from under the fabric being sewn. This is the bobbin thread, which was on to its bobbin before sewing. The bobbin sits in a bobbin case, which is not fixed to the sewing machine case. It floats in its own casing (this is important).

To begin sewing, the needle plunges through the fabric, taking the loop of the top thread with it. Here's the clever bit. A small hook on the bobbin case catches the needle thread. The bobbin case rotates effectively passing the entire bobbin through the loop of top thread. These yarns twist the bobbin thread with the top thread, making the stitch. The needle is then pulled back up. If your thread tension is correct, the twist between the top and bobbin threads is pulled into the fabric you are sewing as it goes.

Once the needle is out of the way, the feed dogs, which are located in the base plate, push the fabric up against the smooth underside of the presser foot. As they then slide backwards, they push the fabric with them to make a visible stitch.

There is also a backstitch lever on the machine. When that is pressed, everything happens as described above except that the feed dogs push the fabric towards you rather than pulling it away from you.

DOUBLE NEEDLE LOCK STITCH MACHINE

This machine is similar to single needle lock stitch machine. But here all components are having two sets i.e. two sets bobbin case, pensioner, take ups, thread guides, spool pin, needle holders. In this the bobbin case are fixed one. The bobbin only taken out from the machine.

This machine adopts two straight needles, vertical- axis rotating hook with self- lubricating feature for catching thread loops and sliding cam take- up to produce two lines of double lock stitch. The needle bar can be engaged and disengaged mechanically and the arm shaft and hook shaft are supported by ball bearing. It is provided with synchronous tooth belt for driving and plunger pump for lubricating and knob-type switch regulator and lever type reverse feeding mechanism. A bobbin thread pull back spring in the bobbin case guarantees the unanimous result of sewing between the bottom thread and upper thread. It is suitable for stitching shirt, uniform, jeans, overcoat or similar clothing.

Types of Sewing

OVER LOCK MACHINE

An over lock stitch sews over the edge of one or two pieces of cloth for edging, hemming or seaming. Usually an over lock sewing machine will cut the edges of the cloth as they are fed through, some are made without cutters. The inclusion of automated cutters allows over lock machine to create finished seams easily and quickly. An over lock sewing machine differs from a lock stitch machine in that it utilizes loopers fed by multiple thread cones rather than a bobbin. Loopers serve to create thread loops that passes from the needle thread to the edges of the fabric so that the edges of the fabric are contained within the seam. Over lock sewing machines usually run at high speeds, from 1000 to 9000 rpm and most are used in industrial setting for edging, hemming and seaming a variety of fabrics and products.

Over lock stitches are extremely versatile as they can be used for decoration, reinforcement, or construction. Over locking is also referred to as “overedging”, “merrowing” or “serging”. Though “serging” technically refers to over locking with cutters, in practice the four terms are used interchangeably.

THE FORMATION OF AN OVER LOCK STITCH

When the needle enters the fabric a loop is formed in the thread at the back of the needle.

As the needle continues its downward motion into the fabric, the lower looper begins its movement from left to right. the tip of the lower looper passes behind the needle and through the loop of thread that has formed behind the needle.

The lower looper continues along its path moving towards the right of the serge. As it moves, the lower thread is carried through the needle thread.

While the lower looper is moving from left to right the upper looper advances from right to left. The tip of the upper looper passes behind the lower looper and picks up the lower looper thread and needle thread.

The lower looper now begins its move back into the far left position. As the upper looper continues to the left, it holds the lower looper thread and needle thread in place.

the needle again begins its downward path passing behind the upper looper and securing the upper lopper thread. This completes the over lock stitch formation and begins the stitch cycle all over again.

DEVELOPMENTS

Following the development of the industrial over lock machines, many companies began competing for the home market. The development and formation of the stitch are similar to the industrial models with some significant exceptions. The home machine sews at approximately 800 stitches per minute (spm) whereas the industrial models sew up to 9500 spm.

Home machines are designed to sew several stitch types whereas the industrial models are designed to sew one type.

Usages of the over lock stitch:

Over lock stitches are typically used for:

- 1-Thread: end-to-end seaming of piece goods for textile finishing.
- 2-thread: finishing seam edges, stitching flat lock seams, stitching elastic and lace to lingerie, and hemming.

- 3-thread: sewing pin tucks, creating narrow rolled hems, finishing fabric edges, decorative edging, and seaming knit or woven fabrics.
- 4-thread: decorative edging and finishing, seaming high-stress areas.
- 5-thread: seam construction in apparel manufacturing.

Some examples of applications are:

- sewing netting
- butt-seaming
- edging emblems
- purl stitching
- decorative edging

Bar tacking machine:

The bar tacking machine has much application in the garment manufacturing industry. One of them is sewing dense tack around the open end of the button hole.

These machines are sewing a number of stitches across the point to be reinforced and then sew covering stitches at right angle over to the first stitches. This variable is the number of tacking stitches and the number of covering stitches.

Some of the bar tacking are fitted with the following special attachments.

Signals are available and it controlled by special mechanism, when the bobbin thread is below a certain level.

Automatic thread cutters are available.

- A pedal which opens and close the work clam.

- This machine is used for the following application in garment industry.

- Closing the end of the button hole.
- Reinforcing the ends of pocket opening.
- To finish the bottom of files.
- Sewing on belt loops.

Button hole sewing machines

Button hole machines are used for making button hole in the garment and to finish the edges and make the button hole in neat finish. These come in a variety of types according to type of button hole needle on the garment. The simplest button hole are used on shirts, blouses & other light weight garment & the more complex one on the heavier tailor garments. The various nesses in button hole machines are from inside button hole. The stitch density whether the button hole is cut before or after sewing & the presents or absence of gimp.

Button hole machine may form a simple circle where the stitches radiate from the center of an eyelet home. 2legs on either side of a straight out with bar tack on both sides as in shirt, a continuous line of sewing of one leg round the end and down the other without the cut as in shank. Button hole on the cups of Jacques a button hole similar in form and larger in length with the hole partially on holy cut and the separate bar tack closing of end a button hole with 2legs and an eyelet hole at one end with a separate bar tack closing of the other end as in front of Jacques overcoats, a variation in which the second leg is sewn over the first stitches of first legs to close the end as frequently on the knit wear and an end as eyelet the edges of which one lightly over sewed known as cut and search which they no more than provide a firm edge to receive a hand sewn button hole in known increasing rate.

The choice between lock stitch and chain stitch is affective by security requirements or hole the finished appeared require and the relative causes are involved. In general button hole on tailor outward make use of the two thread chain stitch the chain effect giving an attractive purl appearance to button hole. The simplest shape of button hole on shirts and other light weight garment is often used with single thread chain stitch and in some cases sewing is done on the inside of the garment.

BUTTON SEWING MACHINE

Without damaging the garment this machine is used to sew the button in the garment but with two holes, four holes or shanks can be sewn on the same machine by simple adjustments to the button clamp and spacing mechanism. The sewing action consists of a series of parallel stitches whose length is equal to the spacing between the centers of the holes. The needle has a vertical movement only and the button is moved from side to side by button clamp.

A button can be sewn on with one or two threads, the number of stitches depending on the type of machine used. Each machine has a maximum number of stitches and can adjust to sew the full amount or half generally decorative button would be sewn on with half the number of stitches used for functional buttons.

Hopper feed is a special attachment which automatically feeds the button to the clamp of needle point of the machine. Here the button and the needle can be automatically positioned and the threads are clipped. Where a neck is required between the under side of the button and the garment the stitch length between the button and the garment is increased and this surplus length can be left as it is or whipped. The whipping operation can incorporate as a second successive operation on a button sewing machine.

BLIND STITCH MACHINE

Blind stitch machine is used to stitch hem in a knitted fabric. As the hem stitch is too small in right side of the garment and it is visible. Sometimes the vision can be set to skip stitch that is to pickup the fabric on alternate stitches only. But this type produces the durability of the stitches.

Zigzag stitches are lock stitches with side to side width as well as stitch length. In mechanical machines basic stitch formation is dictated mainly by a stitch pattern clamp maximum pattern width as established by stitch width regulator. Stitch length is selected for straight stitching and it is same for both stitch types at the same setting but occurs eye as a distance between points and than actual stitch measurement. The clamps built into mechanical machine control stitch formation by means of in their outer edges. A stitch pattern selector positions a finger like follower on appropriate cam. The follower connected to the needle bar cracks those indentations moving the needle from side to side. In most electronic machines the zigzag stitch is programmed by a micro computer which controls movement of stepping motor to direct zigzag movement of needles. Besides a control mentioned most machine have needle position selector which places stitches to left or right of normal position.

FABRIC EXAMINING MACHINE

The fabric examine machine are use to check and examine the fabrics. Through this machine we can inspect the defects like major and minor defects. The machine can be grouped in the following way.

- Manual fabric examine machine
- Semi automatic
- Fully automatic

It has a big inspection table (72" x 30") with light source from top and bottom. The unit if fitted with electronic chokes for instant illumination. It has forward as well as reverse operation and has a variable speed control unit.

There is a foot switch for ease of operation. The unit is fitted with a digital fabric length counter and a digital fault counter. Tensioning device for fabrics is an important feature of the machine along with dual mode operation and continuous checking operation for all types of fabrics.

SPECIAL ATTACHMENTS

Some machine attachment may be supply along with te machine when may be purchased it. Other may be available at additional cast. Attachment make sewing machine easier and provide opportunities for decorative sewing. After deciding which attachments you need get, the dealer to demonstrate the operation of each or the booklets give and instruction for using them. Most of the fabric must be fixed to the presser bar in the place of the presser foot. The attachment that to fast in the presser bar will have prompted similar to presser foot in shade. Some attachment has hook end and that rest on the needle clamp. The attachment most commonly used straight stitch machine.

HEMMERS

Hemmers make hems from three-sixteenths of an inch to seven-eighths of an inch wide, tight on the machine. They really do beautiful work, infinitely more rapid than you could ever expect to do it by hand, and they should be used whenever the material permits.

Machine hemming with the hemmer attachments means hours saved from hand turning and basting. The hem is turned by the hemmer, and at the same time the line of stitching is guided close to the edge of the hem. Always remember, when hemming by machine, to leave threads at the end sufficiently long to thread a hand needle and fasten the end of the hem. Otherwise it is likely to fray.

There are various widths of hems which can be made with hemmers, suitable for the usual requirements. But any hem that is more than seven-eighths of an inch in width must be turned and basted first, and then stitched on the machine in the ordinary way.

RUFFLER

This attachment is capable of taking gathered or pleated frills, and will take and apply frills to another section at the same time. It is useful in making children's clothes and curtains.

It is one of the most valuable attachments in sewing machine, and reflects a great deal of credit upon the inventors of these remarkable time-and-money-saving bits of steel. The method of using the ruffler attachment varies with different machines.

THE BINDER

Another very valuable attachment in your box of sewing-machine attachments is the binder. Of course fine bindings can be made by hand, but the modern, time-saving method is to make them on the sewing-machine with the aid of the rapid little binder. With this tiny bit of mechanical steel you can make ten yards of binding in ten minutes.

This is used for applying ready made or self made bias binding to a straight or curved edge and is a useful attachment for trimming dresses etc.

TUCKER

This is used for making uniform tucks from 1/8 inches to 1 inch in width. Finest pin tucks, or those three-quarters of an inch in width, they can be very easily made without any basting.

CHAPTER II

Sewing Machine Parts

Sewing Machine

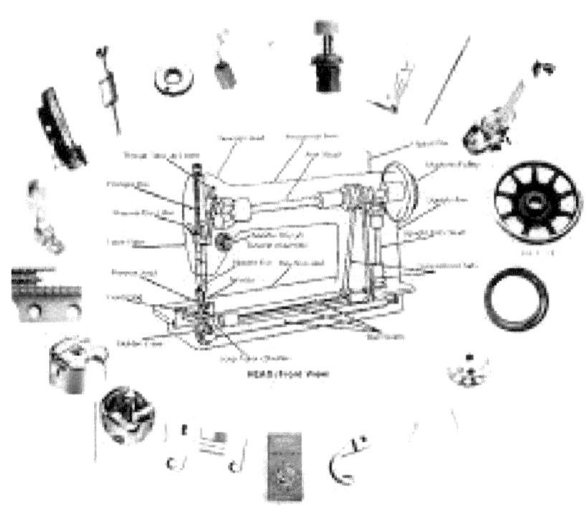

Sewing machine accessories

BOBBIN AND BOBBIN CASE
BOBBIN

Bobbin

A bobbin is a spindle or cylinder with or without flanges on which wire, yarn, thread or film is wound. Bobbins are typically found in sewing machines, cameras. A piece of a sewing machine that holds the bottom threads and is placed in the bobbing case. It generally is under the area the needle penetrates and it loops with the needle threads to form a locked stitch.

BOBBIN CASE

Bobbin Case

It holds the bobbin in position which provides the lower thread and it rotates with the shuttle hook.

Types of Bobbin Case:

1. **Removable Bobbin Case** is used in a single needle machine and can be removed from the machine.
2. **Built in Bobbin Case** is attached with the machine and cannot be removed.

BOBBING WINDING

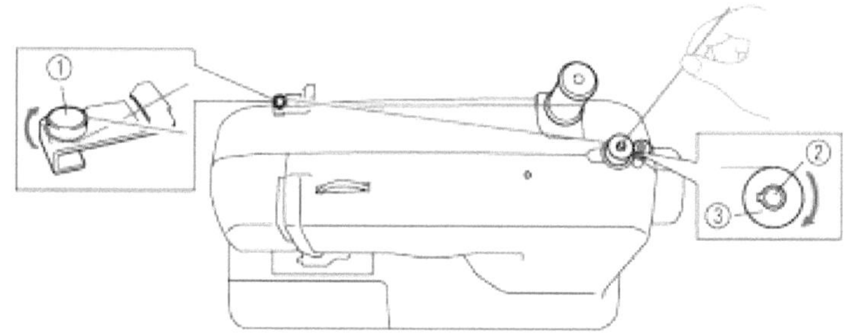

Bobbin winding process

For most machines the thread must be taken out of the needle in order to wind the bobbin. There is normally a bobbin holder on top of the machine. The thread runs from the spool through a sequence of hooks that are specific to the type of machine and on to the spool. The needle is disengaged when the bobbin in winding. This is done automatically or manually, depending on the machine. After the bobbin is wound, the machine is rethreaded, the needle is engaged and the bobbin is placed in its area under a throat plate.

LOOPERS

It is a dull pointed metal piece which has a definite motion cycle to grasp the thread from the needle and helps to form a loop of stitches.

Types of Loopers:

There are two main types of Loopers based on its shape

1. **Eye Looper:**

Eye Looper is used for the machine that has bobbin and bobbin case and used mainly for class 400, class 600 and for all class 500 stitches other than class 501. These types of loopers are carrying the sewing thread through the eye. The two important functions are to grasp the thread from the needle and to interlock the bobbin thread with the needle thread.

1. **Blind Loopers:**

Blind Loopers only do the function of grasping the thread from the needle. It is used for sewing machine without bobbin and bobbin case. Mainly it is used in class 100, 101, 102 and some class 500.

LOOP SPREADER

Loop Spreader is snub massed or dull pointed metal piece which assist the looper in making the stitches. Some blind loopers also have loop spreader. These blind loopers have two dull pointed, the point which grasp the needle thread from the needle is the looper point. The other point which spreads the needle thread loop, which the loop spreader pointed. The action of the loop spreader is coordinate with the loopers. Some machine has multi edged loop spreaders which coordinate with more than one loopers. Some loop spreader is fixed readily, their looper mechanism and parallel to looper action. It is used to form the stitch classes of 400, 500 and 600 stitches.

THREADING FINGER

Threading fingers function in the position of needle above the presser foot shoe. It is a metal link with an eye. These fingers may be static or dynamic. In static links guide the covering thread where as the dynamic links carry thread back and forth across the needle path. It is used to form a 600 class stitches. Thread fingers hooks assist the finger in interlacing its thread between or among the thread of two or more needles in the machine. The action of the thread fingers hooks are synchronized with the thread fingers and needle. Most of the thread fingers mechanism is located in the upper arm of a machine which holds the needle mechanism.

THREADING

UPPER THREADING

Machines vary as how too exactly they are threaded, but all have certain common features. The thread runs from the spool holder, through a tension device and down through the needle. The tension device controls the tension of the thread. It consists of a groove that the thread slides through. The mechanism for setting the tension may be a dial or buttons. With the machine on the left, below, the thread runs from the spool to the hook at the top of the tension area, down the right groove and up the left groove over a little hook and down the left groove again and on to the needle. The dial is turned to set the tension. With the machine on the right below, the thread runs from the spool to a hook at the top of the tension area, down and up the left groove and down the right groove to the needle. The thread runs from the tension device, down to the needle area. There are usually small grooves in the arm that holds the needle, for the thread to pass through. This holds the thread close to the needle arm. The thread then runs down to and through the eye of the needle.

LOWER THREADING

Once the bobbin is in place and the machine is threaded, generally turn the wheel of the machine while holding the needle thread of to the side. This will bring down the needle. The needle pass down through the throat plate and the needle thread will catch the bobbin thread and pull it up through the throat plate when comes back up again.

Stitching auxiliaries are not carrying the thread but it helps the formation of perfect stitches. There are three types of stitching auxiliaries available.

- **Knife:** It trims the edges of the fabric before sewing and it can be found in over lock machines.
- **Positioner:** Before stitching the materials are positioned by this type of positioner.
- **Piercing:** It pierce the fabric before stitching and it is used in the button hole machine to form a button hole.

THROAT PLATE

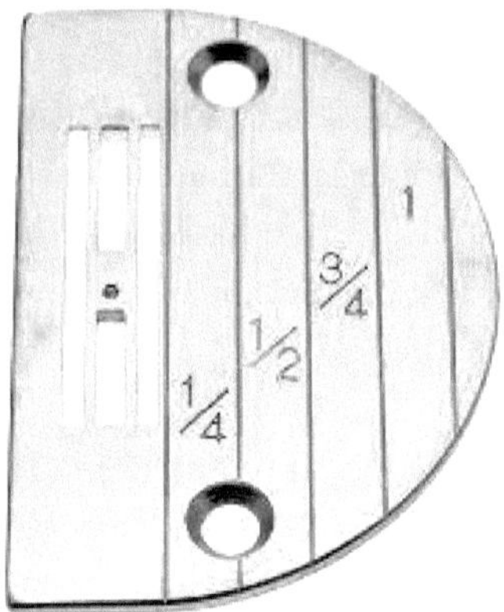

Throat Plate

The throat plate covers the area that holds the bobbin. It has an opening for the needle to pass through, as well as lines that serve as sewing guides. The needle may be a single hole or an oblong hole which allows the needle to make stitches that have width such as zigzag stitches.

TENSION GUIDE

Tension refers to the force that is applied by the machine on your thread. You can also effect tension by the amount of pull or push you apply to the fabric as you feed it through under the needle- you should not apply force. Instead, just use your hands to guide the fabric through. Let the feed dogs actually feed the fabric through.

Thread Tension guide

There are two ways in which you can adjust tension. The upper thread(needle thread- coming from the spool) and the bobbin thread each have tension.

Types of tension device

1. Direct- it has two canvas disc, tension spring and tension screw to provide tension to thread
2. Indirect- these are cylindrical and conical in shape with a hook which is placed over the tension disc to provide extra tension.
3. Auxiliary- these are placed somewhere between the actual tension disc and needle to provide extra tension to the thread.

THREAD TAKE UP

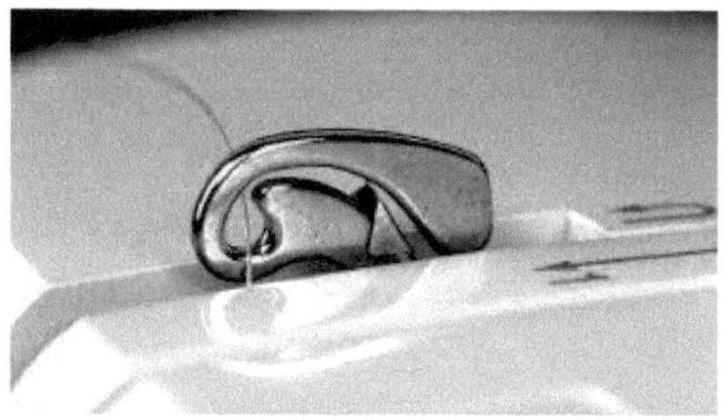

Thread take up lever

After the bobbin hook contacts the needle thread, the threads is pulled up in order to make the stitch tight and this action is done by the take up lever. It also helps the bobbin hook to receive the thread freely and quickly.

Types of take up levers

- Oscillating levers
- Rotating levers

Oscillating levers

It is used in a single needle machine and the gap will be 1" for oscillating of take up lever.

Rotating levers

This type lever which rotate to provide the thread looser and tighter.

PRESSER FOOTER

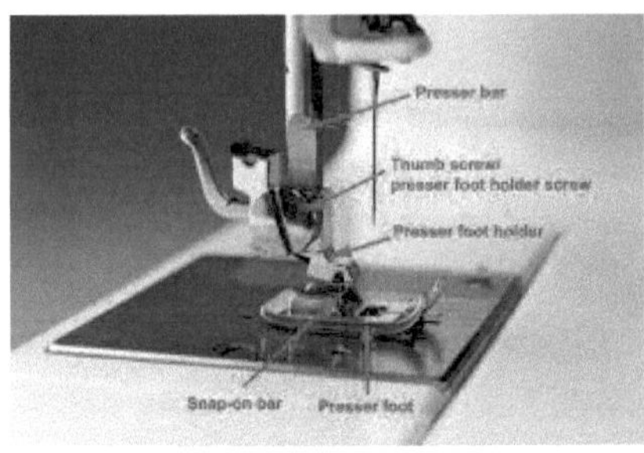

Presser footer

The presser foot can be raised and lowered with a small lever at the back of, or beside, the needle. When up, it allows free movement of the fabric. When down, it presses the cloth against a base plate. The base plate has a couple of textured moving parts (the feed dogs) that keeps the material moving past the needle at an even rate. (You can sew with the presser foot up, but you tend to get very uneven stitches. This is because you have to move the fabric yourself, and keeping it moving at an even rate is almost impossible).

Presser feet hold down the fabric and help guide it through. They also serve various special functions. E.g. of special feet are the rolled hem foot, which causes the fabric to roll and the appliqué foot, which has the opening in the back to allow the bulk of the satin stitch to pass through. Other special feet that are commonly include zipper and button hole foot. Knowing what types are available and when to use them can make all the difference in the quality of your work. These special feet also take a lot of the frustration out of sewing. Special sewing function can be performed using other specialty feet such as: appliqué foot, bias binder, pin tuck feet, felling foot, cording foot, special hemmers and many more.

FEEDING MECHANISM

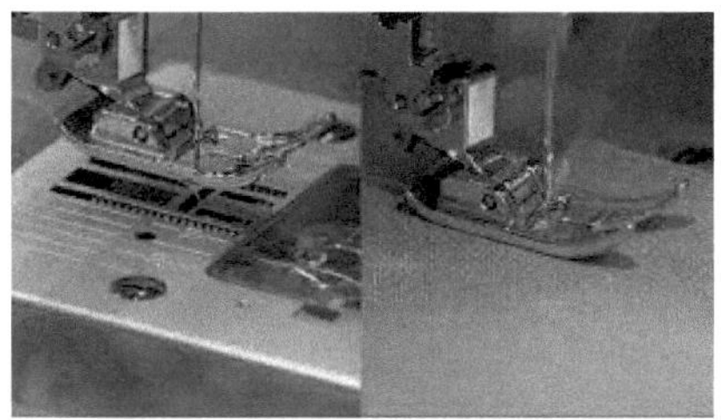

Sewing Machine feeder

In a sewing machine, the feeder mechanism which is typically used to pull fabric through a sewing mechanism. A set of feed dogs typically resemble two or three short, thin metal bars, cross cut with diagonal furrows, which move back and forth in grooves slightly larger than the bars. The type of motion used(forward, then down, then backwards, then up) serves to pull the fabric through,

since the " dogs" are in contact with the material on the forward stroke, and are pulled down below the main plate on the back ward stroke by the sewing machine's mechanism. The result is that, between stitches, the fabric is pulled along in discrete steps.

Most sewing machines using feed dogs can pull fabric forward or backwards at various stitch lengths; this is typically controlled by a stitch lever on the front of the machine.

Types of feed mechanism

Based on the end use and application the feed mechanism can be classified in the following types.

- Manual feed or free motion or free hand or darning feed
- Drop feed
- Differential feed
- Needle feed
- Compound feed
- Unison feed
- Puller, roller feed
- Cup feed

Manual feed or free motion or free hand or darning feed

- The operator moves work under needle. Free hand motion.
- Machine may have a vertical motion foot that clamps the foot before the needle enters the material, and releases to allow the operator to manipulate the goods between each stitch.
- Darning, embroidery, free hand quilting etc.

CHAPTER III

Sewing Threads

SEWING NEEDLE

The way in which fabric is penetrated by the needle during sewing has a direct effect on seam strength and on garment appearance and wearable life.

TYPES OF SEWING NEEDLES

Hand sewing needles

1. Sewing needle

    a. standard
    b. long

2. Embroidery needle

    a. pointed
    b. round

3. Darning needle

Machine sewing needle

1. Round pointed needle

    - Set point
    - Ball point

2. Cutting point needle

1. HAND SEWING NEEDLE

For hand sewing, needle should be large enough to carry the thread easily. If a needle that is too small it will cut the thread, and too- large needle may tear the cloth. For basting we suggest the long needle used my milliners.

The needles commonly used in dress making are called sharps. In your sewing basket you should keep a supply of sharps nos. 5, 6,7,8,9 and 10. for very heavy work use nos. 5 and 6 with threads 20 to 40. Use needles 7 and 8 for threads nos. 60 to 90 and needles 9 and 10 for threads nos. 100 to 150.

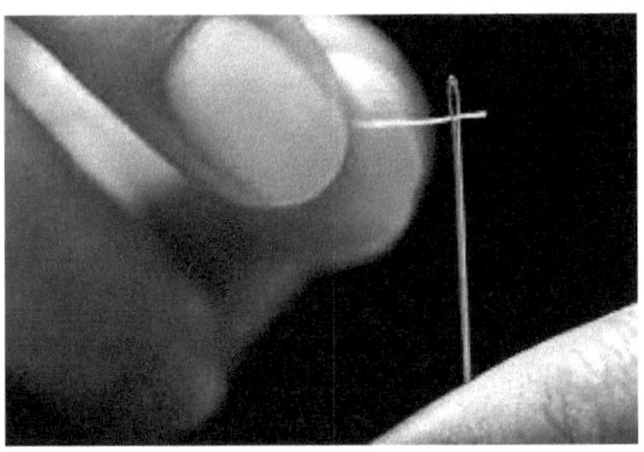

Hand Sewing Needle

2. MACHINE NEEDLE

All sewing machine needles have the same basic parts. The variation in needle causes by the shape of the parts and the length of the parts.

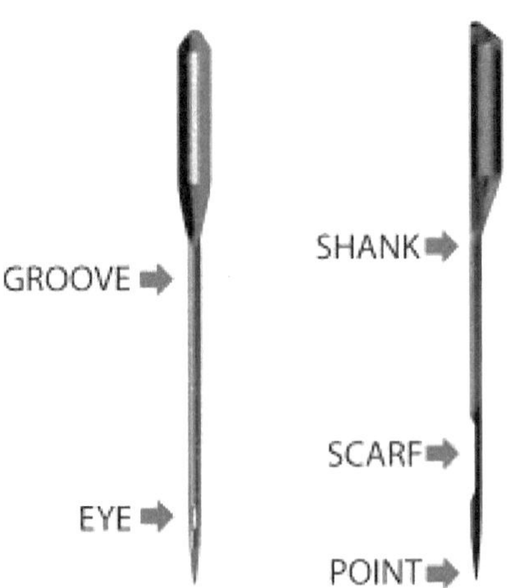

Machine Needle and its parts

The function of the sewing machine needle is general are:

- To produce a hole in the material for the thread to pass through and to do so without causing any damage to the material.
- To carry the needle thread through the material and there form a loop which can be picked up by the hook on the bobbin case in a lock stitch machine or by the looper or other mechanism in machine.
- To pass the needle thread through the loop formed by the lopper mechanism on the machines other than lock stitch.

Shank

- The upper thick part of a sewing machine needle is called the shank. This part of the needle is inserted in the machine. Home sewing machine needles are composed of a flat and a round side, to assist in always having the needle in the correct position.
- Always refer your sewing machine manual for the correct way to insert the needle in your machine.
- Industrial sewing machines have a completely round shaft and the groove is used to know which direction to put a new needle in the machine.

Shaft

- The shaft of the sewing machine needed is the area from the bottom of the shank to the point. The shaft contains the groove, scarf, eye and point of the needle.

Groove

- The groove is in the side of the needle leading to the eye. The groove is the place for the thread to lay into the needle.
- Use your finger nail and feel the groove of the needle on various sizes to understand why a different size thread would be needed for heavier thread.

Scarf

- The scarf is a groove out of one side of the needle. The scarf allows the bobbin case hook to intersect with the upper thread and form stitches.

Eye

- The eye of the needle carries the thread so the machine can keep forming stitches.
- The size of the eye can vary and works in conjunction with the groove of the needle.
- Using a needle with an eye that is too small or too large can cause a needle to shred and break.

Point

- The point of the needle is the first contact with the fabric and responsible for how the needle pierces the fabric.
- The most common type of points is sharps, ball point and universal.

Types of Needles

- **Sharp needles** are for all woven fabrics. The sharp point is especially helpful in sewing straight lines and tasks such as tops stitching.
- **Ball point needles** are designed for knit fabric so that the point glides between the loops of a knit fabric without disturbing the fibers that make up the fabric. Ball point needles do not form as straight stitching as sharp needles. The non straight stitching is more apt to stretch with the fabric.
- **Universal needles** can be used with woven or knit fabric. The point of the universal needle is sharp yet very slightly rounded giving it the characteristic of a sharp and a ball point needle.

CHAPTER IV

Sewing & Spreading

CUTTING

The use of the term cutting can present a difficulty. It is used in the sense of 'cutting room', an area which normally includes the activities of marker planning, spreading and preparation for sewing as well as being used to refer to actual cutting of garment parts from the lay.

1. **Precision of cut**

Garments cannot be assembled satisfactorily, and then may not fit the body correctly, if they have not been cut accurately to the pattern shape. The ease with which accuracy is achieved depends on the method of cutting employed and in some cases on the marker planning and marker making. In manual cutting using a knife, accuracy of cut, given good line definition depends on appropriate well maintained cutting knifes and on the skill and motivation of the cutter. In the both the cutting and computer- controlled cutting, the achievement of accuracy comes for the equipment.

1. **Clean edges**

The raw edge of the fabric should not show fraying or snagging. Such defects come from an imperfectly sharpened knife.

3. **Unscorched, unfused edges**

The build -up of heart in the knife blade comes from the friction of the blade passing through the fabric. This, in extreme cases, leads to scorching of the fabric and more frequently to the fusing of the raw edges of thermoplastic fiber fabrics, such as those containing polyamide or polyester. The cutter cannot separate individual plies from the pile of cut parts. Forced separation causes snagged edges and on any case, the hard edge is uncomfortable in wear. Solutions to this problem lie in a well- sharpened blade, a blade with a wavy edge, the use of anti- fusion paper during spreading, spraying the blade and reducing the height of the lay.

4. **Support of the lay**

The cutting system must provide means not only to support the fabric but also to allow the blade to penetrate the lower ply of a spread and server all the fibers.

5. **Consistent cutting**

The cutting system should not be limited in the height or plies it will cut, because of progressive deterioration in cutting quality, though there may be mechanical or human reasons, such as topping or leaning for the height of lay being limited.

METHODS OF CUTTING

Majority of cutting rooms today, the cutting process makes use of the hand shears, a mechanized knife blade is one of the several possible types or a die press which stamps out the garment shapes.

1. Hand shears
2. Straight knife
3. Band knife
4. Round knife
5. Die cutters
6. Notches
7. Drills and thread marker
8. Computer control cutting knife
9. Laser cutting
10. Plasma cutting
11. Water jet cutting
12. Ultrasonic cutting

HAND SHEARS

Hand shears is normally used when cutting only a single or double plies. The lower blade of the shears passes under the plies but the subsequent distortion of the fabric is only temporary and accurate cutting to the line can be achieved with practice. Left- handed shears are available since the cutting line will not easily be seen if right handed shears are used by a left handed person. This method is flexible enough to accommodate any fabric construction and pattern shape. The obvious disadvantage of any method lies in the time it consumes and the consequent high labor cost per garment, but it appropriate for made- to- measure garments.

CUTTING TOOLS AND EQUIPMENTS

1. **Scissors**

These have round handles and the blades are usually less than 6”. They are designed mainly for snipping thread and trimming seams. However, scissors with 5” blade can be used by beginners for cutting fabric as well. For embroidery and for cutting button holes sharp pointed scissors with blades ½” to 1” long are useful the best types of scissors have blades of uneven width. They should be held so that the wider blade is above the narrower blade.

2. **Dress makers shears**

For cutting fabric, shears are more satisfactory than scissors. Shears differ from scissors in that they have one small ring handle for thumb and a large ring handle for the second, third and fourth fingers. They also have longer blades.

3. **Pinking shears**

These are useful for finishing the edges of seams and other raw edges of fabric. They produce a notched cutting line which prevents raveling of firmly woven fabrics. Pinking gives neat appearance to the inside of the garment.

4. **Button hole scissors**

These can be adjusted so as to cut buttonholes in any size you require. They are useful if you are an expert in tailoring and need to make many buttonholes.

STRAIGHT KNIFE CUTTING MACHINE

The straight knife cutting machine consists of a base plate, an up right stand to hold the vertical blade, motor, a handle for moving assembly, a sharpening device and a handle to transfer the whole assembly from one place to another.

Two kinds of power are required to operate a straight knife. Motor power drives the reciprocating blade and operator power drives the knife through the lay. Normally available blade heights vary from 10 cm to 33 cm and normally available strokes vary from 2.5 to 4.5 cm. the greater the blade cuts the fabric and more easily the operator can move the machine.

The most important consideration is selecting a straight knife is the power required from the operator to move the knife is the power required from the operator to move the knife is the power required for the operator to move the knife through the lay. Operator effort is affected by the weight of the motor, the shape of the stand, handle height, stroke, sharpness of blade and the base plate movement.

The normal blade has a straight edge that varies from coarse to fine depending upon the type of fabric being cut. Wavy edged knifes are used to reduce the heat generation and hence can be used for cutting synthetic materials without fusing difficulties. The speed of the blades can also be adjusted by having variable speed mechanism.

The straight knife is a common means of cutting lays in conventional cutting rooms because it is versatile, portable than a band knife and easy to maintain. Even if a band knife is used for main cutting operation a straight knife will be used to separate the lay into sections for easier handling.

BAND KNIFE CUTTING MACHINE

A band knife comprises a series of three or more pulleys powered by an electric motor. With a continuously rotating steel blade mounted on then, one edge of the blade is sharpened. The principle of operation is different from a straight knife, in that the band knife passes through a slot in the cutting table, in a fixed position and the section of lay to be cut is moved past it. The blade is usually narrower than straight knife.

Band knives are used when a higher standard or cutting accuracy is required that can be obtained with a straight knife. Space must be left around garment parts when marking so that they can be cut from the lay using a straight knife and then cut exactly using the band knife.

When small parts such as collars, cuffs and pockets are cut, a template of metal or fiber board in the shape of the pattern piece may be clamped to the section of lay on top of the marking which is then drawn past the band knife blade, cutting exactly along the hard edge. Band knife cutting machines are used more in men's wear than in women's wear and are often used to cut large garment parts such as the large panels of jackets and over coats.

ROUND KNIFE CUTTING MACHINE

The elements of a round knife cutting machine are a base plate, above which is mounted on electric motor, a handle for the cutter to direct the blade and a circular blade rotating so that the leading edge cuts downwards into the fabric. Blade diameters vary from 6cm to 20cm. round knives are not suitable for cutting curved lines in high lays because the blade does not strike all the plies simultaneously at the same point as vertical blade does. Therefore a round knife is used only for straight lines or lower lays of relatively few plies. It is naturally much more difficult for a circular blade to cut a tight curve, such as an arm hole.

DIE CUTTERS

In contrast to the fast moving blades used in the methods of cutting previously described, die cutting involves pressing rigid blade through the lay of the fabric. The die called a clicker in the shoe industry is a knife in the shape of a pattern periphery, including notches. One or more tie bars secure its stability. Free standing dies generally fall into two categories. They can be of strip steel, manufactured by bending the strip to the shape required and welding the joint. These caccot be sharpened and must be replaced when worn. Alternatively, they can be heavier gauge, forged dies which can be re- sharpened but which are about five times the price of strip steel. The position of the tie bars determines the depth of curt which is generally greater with forged dies.

The die press generally has a cutting arm supported by a single pillar at the back of the machine; it swings to the side to allow the placing of dies on top of the fabric. The downward cutting stroke of the press should be so controlled that the edge of the die just penetrates the cutting pad or surface in order that the fibers of the lowest ply are completely separated. Die presses are of two types: impact which makes a single press on the die, and, more commonly, hytronic which exerts continuous pressure on the die until it has cut the fabric and made contact with the soft metal or nylon pad. Once the pad, after repeated cutting, reaches an unsatisfactory state of wear, its surface is re-cut and re-leveled. For die cutting the spreader spreads a lay to the required number of plies and may place a marker on top to guide the placement of dies. The spread is cut into sections to allow transport to the cutting pad. In some cases, no marker is used the operator placing the dies by eye to eye to the correct grain line and as close together as this method allows.

One important disadvantage of die cutting is its greater use of fabric. When the die press forces the die press forces the dies through the fabric it also forces a borrow wedge of fabric between the dies. The narrow wedge exists because the sharpened cutting edge of the die is necessarily of narrower gauge than the top of the die. Thus if the dies are butted together they touch at the top but show a small gap at the level of the cutting edges. The action of the press will compress this narrow wedge of fabric to the point where it will rupture the dies. Hence it is necessary to leave a significant gap between two dies, say 2 to 3 mm. similarly a single die will not cut satisfactorily if placed closer than 3 to 4 mm to a previously cut edge. Large area die cutting presents a number of technical problems. A complete lay of free dies several meters long on top of the fabric could be cut by a twin pillar or four pillar presses extending across the lay. For economic and engineering reasons the depth of the press is limited.

NOTCHES

Many garment parts require that notches are cut into the edges of them to enable alignment during sewing with other garment parts. The previous four methods of cutting can be used to cut notches, but accuracy depends of the operator. Specialized notching equipment provides greater accuracy because a guide lines up the notcher with the cut edge. Both straight notches and vee notches are available. A further machine the hot notcher, incorporates a heating element in order that the blade may slightly scorch the fibers adjacent to the natch in order to prevent it fraying and disappearing. This cannot be used with thermoplastic fibers or certain unlinrd garments. One fabric requiring it may be loosely woven tweed.

DRILLS AND THREAD MARKER

Where reference marks are needed away from the edge of a garment part, such as for the position of pockets, darts and similar features, a hole is often drilled through all the plies of fabric on the lay. The drill mounting includes a motor, a base plate with a hole to allow the drill to pass through and a spirit level to ensure that the base is horizontal and hence the drill vertical.

On many fabrics the drill is used cold and the hole remains visible until the sewing operator comes to use it. On looser weave fabrics where the hole may close up, a hot drill is used, which will slightly scorch or fuse the edges of the hole.

A hypodermic drill may also be used which leaves a small deposit of paint on each ply of fabric. If it is important that no mark remains on the fabric, a long thread may be passed through the lay which in then cut with scissors between each ply, leaving a few centimeters visible on each garment panel. All drill holes must eventually be concealed by the construction of the garment.

SPREADING

The objective of spreading is to place the number of plies of fabric that the production planning process has dictated, to the length of themarker plan, in the colours required, correctlyalignedas to length and width, and withouttension. There are number of prices to be paid for this saving in the time and cost of cutting and the cost of materials.

First, the spreading of multi-size lays of many plies demands strongly constructed tables, usually with steel legs and braced frames, a heavy laminated, smooth wood top, and sometimes centre legs. A 10 meter lay of shirting fabric with 200 plies can weigh up to 6000 kg and with 150 cm wide fabric can exert a downward pressure of up to approximately 40kg per square meter on the table surface. The table may also bear the weight of a spreading machine, traveling on steel rails at the edge of the table. The type of table surface is critical for the spreading and cutting operations. Second, spreading is itself a time-consuming operation. With the highest lays it can consume more time in total than cutting, especially if the cutting is by computer-controlled knife. Just as with the marking and cutting operations, the efforts of engineers have sophisticated equipment designed to reduce spreading time and make the operation more automatic.

A study of spreading must include the following considerations:

1. The requirements of the spreading process.
2. Methods of spreading
3. The nature of fabric packages.

THE REQUIREMENTS OF THE SPREADING PROCESS

Spreading must achieve a number of specific objectives:

1. Shade sorting of cloth pieces

Lays commonly require more than one roll of cloth and lays which include several colours normally require more than one roll of each colour to achieve enough plies in total. It is likely that cloth pieces that are nominally the same colour will have been dyed separately and are not an exact shade match. A garment made from parts cut from these different pieces would be likely to show a shaded effect between its different panels. Thus when deliveries of a number of rolls of cloth of the same colour are received,they should be sorted into batches such that shade differences between them are undetectable.

2. Correct ply direction and adequate lay stability

These two factors must be considered together as the opportunities for achieving them are related. They depend on fabric type, pattern shape and the spreading equipment that is available.

Methods if spreading which lay alternate plies in different directions can only are used for either way fabrics. In this case the pattern pieces can face in either direction in the marker and the following opportunities are available:

a. for symmetrical pattern pieces, and fabric which is suitable spread face to face, the fabric can be spread along face up immediately back again face down.
b. For symmetrical as well as symmetrical pattern pieces, and fabric which is stable spread all the same way up, the fabric can be spread along and immediately back again but the roll must be turned on a turntable before returning.
c. For asymmetrical as well as symmetrical pattern pieces, and fabric which is stable all the same way up, the spreader spreads in one direction only and 'dead heads' back to spread the next ply in the same direction.
d. For symmetrical pattern pieces, and fabric which is stable face to face, the spreader spreads in one direction only but after 'dead handling' back ,a turntable is required to rotate the roll before the next ply is spread in the same direction.

3) Alignment of plies:

Every ply should compromise at least the length and width of the marker plan, but should have the minimum possible extra outside those measurements.

4) Correct ply tension:

If the plies are spread with too slack a tension they will lie in ridges with irregular fullness. If plies are spread in a stretched state they will maintain their tension while held in the lay, but will contract after cutting or during sewing, thus shrinking the garment parts to a smaller size than the pattern pieces. In a non stretch fabric practically all elongation of the fabric occurs in such a manner that rapid relaxation and recovery ensures.

5) Elimination of fabric faults:

Fabric faults (flows, holes, stains, etc.,) may be identified by the fabric supplier, and additional faults may be detected during examination of the fabric by the garment manufacturer prior to spreading.

6) Elimination of static electricity:

In spreading plies of fabric containing man-made fibres, friction may increase the charge of static electricity in the fabric. Friction may be reduced by changing the method of threading the fabric through the guide bars of the spreading machine. Humidity in the atmosphere of the cutting room may also be increased, thus allowing the static electricity to discharge continuously through the atmosphere.

7) Avoidance of distortion in the spread

A layer of glazed paper, laid glazed side down, is normally placed at the bottom of the spread. This helps to avoid disturbing the lowest plies of material in the spread when the base plate of a straight knife passes underneath, and also gives stability to the lay if it is to be moved on a floatation table. In addition, it prevents snagging of the fabric on the table surface which often becomes roughened with use.

8) Avoidance of fusion of plies during cutting:

Cut edges of thermoplastic fibre fabrics may fuse together during cutting if the cutting knife becomes hot as a result of friction with the fabric. In this case, anti-fusion paper may be used in the same way as interleaving paper. It contains a lubricant which lubricates the knife blade as it passes through the spread, thus reducing the increase in temperature of the blade arising from friction.

METHODS OF SPREADING:

The methods of spreading which the industry uses can be divided into:

1. Spreading by hand
2. Spreading using a traveling machine

classified by application

- Semi automatic
- Fully automatic

SPREADING BY HAND:

It is time consuming method, requiring an operator at each side of the table. The fabric is drawn from its package which, if it is a roll, may be supported on a frame, and carried along the table where the end is secured by weights or a clamp. The operators work back from the end, aligning the edges and ensuring that there is no tension and that there are no wrinkles.

The ply is normally cut with hand shears or with a powered circular knife mounted on a frame, though a few fabrics are ripped at the end of the ply to discover the exact weft grain and enable some straightening of a slightly crooked fabric to take place. Typical fabrics which must be spread by hand are checks, crosswise strips and other regularly repeating patterns, as well as those with a repeating design at intervals of a permanent length. If accurate 'stacking up' of the design vertically through the spread is necessary, the fabric may be 'spiked' on to a series of sharp spikes set vertically on the spreading table.

SPREADING USING A TRAVELLING MACHINE:

Spreading machines carry the piece of fabric from end to end of the spread, dispensing one ply at a time onto the spread. Their basic elements consist of a frame carriage, wheels traveling in guide rails at the edge of the table, a fabric support, and guide collars to aid the correct unrolling of the fabric. In the simpler versions, the operator clamps the free end of fabric in line with the end of the spread, pushes the spreader to the other end, cuts off the ply in line with that end, clamps the beginning of the next ply, pushes the spreader to the other end and so on.

More advanced spreading machines may include a motor to drive the carriage, a platform on which the operator rides, a ply-cutting device with automatic catcher to hold the ends of the ply in place, a ply counter, an alignment shifter actuated by photo electric edge guides, a turntable and a direct drive on the fabric support, synchronized with the speed of travel, to reduce or eliminate tension in the fabric being spread.

The advent of microprocessor control has enabled the development of more automatic functions on spreading machines. Thus a spreader can be pre-set to a selected number of plies, emitting an audible signal when it has reached the selected number or has come to the end of piece of fabric. Automatic turn tabling gives automatic spreading even for corduroys which are normally spread face to face. With robotic spreading, when the piece is finished the spreader returns to an auto lifter at the end of the table transfers the empty centre bar to the lifter which then advances the next piece to the spreader. It repeats the process until it achieves the required number of plies. This method requires automatic sensing of previously marked flaws and damages.

Marking Tool

MARKER

It is useful to break marker making down into:

- Marker Planning or the placement of pattern piece to meet technical requirements and the needs of material economy, and
- Marker utilization which may include drawing the marker plan directly onto fabric drawing it onto a paper marker by pen or automatic plotter or where the cutting method allows it, regarding pattern piece information on the paper marker or on the fabric without actually drawing pattern lines on it. Provision may have to be made for the same marker plan to be used many times.

THE REQUIREMENTS OF MARKER PLANNING:

Industry has always paid great attention to marker planning, because when the cutting room cuts cloth it spends around of the companies turnover. Any reduction in the amount of cloth used per garment leads to increased profit.

Marker planning is a conceptualizing, intuitive, open and creative process, in contrast to making up a jigsaw puzzle, which is an analytical, step-by-step and closed process. There is no final solution to a marker planning problem, only a more tightly packed and therefore shorter marker the more time is spent on it. The work of the marker planner is subject to a number of constraints. These relate to

1. the nature of the fabric and the desired result in the finished garment
2. requirements of quality in cutting
3. requirements of production planning

THE NATURE OF THE FABRIC AND THE DESIRED RESULT IN THE FINISHED GARMENT

a. **Pattern alignment in relation to the grain of the fabric:**

Pattern pieces normally carry a grain line. When pattern pieces are laid down the piece of cloth, as is commonest with large pattern pieces, the grain line should lie parallel to the line of the warp in a woven fabric or the Wales in a knitted fabric. Where pattern pieces are laid across the piece, the grain line should lie parallel to the weft or course direction. In bias cutting, which is often used in large pattern pieces as part of the garment style in ladies dresses and lingerie, as well as in small pattern pieces such as satisfactory garment assembly, the grain lines will (normally) be at 45to the warp.

a. **Symmetry and asymmetry**

Many fabrics can be turned round (though 180^0) and retain the same appearance and these are designed 'either way' or 'asymmetrical'. In this case, if a fabric ply is turned round it does not retain the same appearance, especially when the two opposite ways are sewn together.

c. **The design characteristics of the finished garment**

For example if a vertical stripe does not show a complete mirror image repeat, the right and left sides of a garment may be designed to be mirror images of each other. In this case, a marker is planned which uses a half set of patterns, and the required effect is created in the spreading of fabric which places pairs face to face.

THE REQUIREMENTS OF QUALITY IN CUTTING:

a. For the majority of cutting situations where a knife blade is used, the placements of the pattern pieces in the marker most give freedom of knife movement and not restrict the path of the knife so that it leads to inaccurate cutting. A blade, which has width, cannot turn a perfect right angle in the middle of a pattern piece and space must always be allowed for a knife to turn such corners. Also, in practice, a curved part of a pattern such a sleeve head, when placed abutting a straight edge or the crown of the curve being straightened. The amount of space which must be left will depend on the actual cutting method employed.

b. Correct labeling of cut garment parts is essential if, in sorting and bundling a multi-size lay after cutting, operators are to identify correctly the parts which make up the whole garment sizes. It is the responsibility of the marker planner to code every pattern piece with its size as the marker is planned.

THE REQUIREMENTS OF PRODUCTION PLANNING

When an order is placed for a quality of garments, it normally specifies a quantity of each size and colour, the former often given as ratio. The requirements of production planning and control will be to supply the sewing room with an adequate amount of cut garments at sufficiently frequent intervals, consistent with availability of fabric and the best utilization of cutting room resources. Among the latter considerations is that, for a given quantity of garments, a high lay rather than a low lay gives a lower cutting time which is important if the sewing room requires the cut work urgently. The shorter lay will also require a shorter marker.

EFFICIENCY OF THE MARKER PLAN

The marker planner measures his success by the efficiency of the marker plan created. A formula describes this

Area of patterns in the marker plan

--- X 100%

Total Area of the marker plan

Since the reduction in fabric cost is so important, the company expects the planner to discover opportunities for improvements in marker efficiency by suggesting alterations to patterns and cloth, the two elements brought in market planning. The first sort of opportunities is commonly designated pattern engineering. Chief among these is an examination of seam location to ensure the best possible placement of patterns in the marker. In one case shift of a seam might allow the placement of small parts in areas otherwise wasted, for instance in the armhole of a jacket or shirt lying next to the edge of a marker. In another case the seam is moved to enable the better placement of large panels across the whole width of the fabric.

The second sort of opportunity arises in the influence of the marker planners has on the selection of fabric widths where a choices available. The 'best' width among other factors on the costs of various fabric widths per sq.m, the typical number of sizes in a marker, the potential pattern engineering changes at various widths and the marker efficiency of a series of test markers.

METHODS OF MARKER PLANNING AND MARKER:

The **methods of marker**are basically classified into two categories.

1. Manual marker
2. Computerised marker

But say about, the **marker type** can be classified into two types

i. Paper marker
ii. Fabric marker

MANUAL MARKER PLANNING WITH FULL SIZE PATTERNS:

Prior to the development of computerized marker planning systems, all markers were planned by working with full size pattern. For many companies in the industry this method is till used, because the more modern alternatives are expensive, and because these companies make only short or single size markers and the planner can see the whole of the plan relatively easily. Thc plannsr words by moving around the full size patterns until a satisfactory plan is obtained.

In a few clothing companies this planning is done directly on the fabric to be cut and the pattern shapes marked in immediately. This can only be done when the length of the marker is predictable and in marking directly on to fabric, the necessary accurate reproduction of the pattern and good definition of line can be difficult to achieve. Patterns are usually made from card and it is important that the edges do not become worn and that the pattern is held firmly while drawing takes place. Various chalk or wax materials can be used to draw with but whatever is used needs to be easily held and readily sharpened. The quality of the line also depends on the surface nature of the fabric.

This method takes considerable skill to achieve accuracy an it takes considerable time, but it is economical for single garments and also for check fabric since it allows the patterns to be manipulated during the marking process. In many companies,more than one lay is cut using the same marker plane. If the plan is drawn directly on to the fabric, this process of drawing round the patterns has to repeated for each lay.

It is much more common for a paper marker to be used for cutting and in this case the pattern lines and style and size information are usually drawn on spot and cross paper to ensure adherence to grain lines. It is still essential that patterns do not become worn but the satisfactorily fine line is easier to achieve that than when marking directly on to fabric as a pencil or a ball point pen can be used. Again, multiple copies of the paper marker are normally needed. These copies can either be made when the marker plan is first drawn, or the master marker can be reproduced as needed by a verity of methods.

MARKER DUPLICATING:

Again, multiple copies of the paper marker are normally needed. These copies can either be made when the marker plan is first drawn, or the master marker can be reproduced as needed by a variety of methods.

There are different duplicating systems available

a. Carbon duplicating
b. Spirit duplicating or hectograph carbon system
c. Di - azo photographic method

d. Perforated marker

e. **Carbon duplicating :**

For copies to be made as the original is drawn and where small numbers of copies only are needed, use can be made of carbon paper, usually double sided, or the same effect can be achieved with special NCR-Type paper. In either case, 6-8 copies can be made without too great a deterioration in the fitness of the line.

b. **Spirit duplicating or hectograph carbon system:**

In this process, the master marker is drawn on paper with the layer of special hectograph paper underneath it. This paper transfers a blue line on to the back of the master as it is drawn. The master is then used to make one copy at a time in a duplicating machine. The machine uses alcohol to wet a plain white paper which is then passed with the master between two rollers, transferring the lines on to the copy. It is a messy process but many copies can be produced.

c. **Di azo photographic method:**

This process makes as many copies of the marker as are needed, one at a time, following the drawing of a master marker. The master marker and a light-sensitive paper are passed under high intensity ultra-violet light and the light sensitive paper is developed using ammonia vapour. The lines remain visible. It is a clean process which can make unlimited number of copies with good definition and it must be used with ample ventilation to remove ammonia fumes. The paper is expensive but the equipment is comparatively cheap.

d. **Perforated marker:**

An alteration method of paper marker is perforated marker from the initial hand drawn version by means of a punch perforator. This has been used in the clothing industry but is more commonly used for cutting, upholstery fabrics.

COMPUTERISED MARKER PLANNING:

This method is normally part of an integrated system which includes digitizing or scanning of full size patterns into the computer, facilities for pattern adaptation, and by in putting appropriate great rules, the means to generate all the sizes required. The planner uses a visual display unit with keyboard, tabled and data pen, puck or mouse.

The planner specifies the exact make up of the marker plan; the width of the fabric, the pattern pieces to be used, the sizes to be included and all constraints to be applied, including any matching of checks. The system produces the marker plan automatically or interactively. Automatic marker planning involves calling up data defining the placement of pieces in markers previously planned, and selecting from a series, that marker conformation which gives the highest marker efficiency.

Interactive marker planning is more common and is the process by which the operator plans markers by interacting directly with the system through the VDU screen. All the pattern pieces are displayed in miniature at the top of the screen. In the middle of the screen are two horizontal lines defining the marker width and a vertical line at the left representing the beginning of the marker. The right end is for the moment open. At the bottom of the screen is written marker identification, with marker length and efficiency constantly updated during the planning proves.

The data pen, tablet and the computer keyboard are used to manipulate the pattern pieces. A combination of movements of the pen and commands via the key board enable pattern pieces to be moved about the screen and positioned in the marker. The system finally positions the pattern pieces precisely according to the marking rule specified. After selecting the most economical marker plan devised in the time available, the computer will provide an accurate piece count; calculate a marker plan efficiency, percentage and total length of the pattern peripheries. When the marker plan is complete it will be store in a marker plan file for future retrieval.

The quality of marker planning is more consistent than with manual methods, because instructions regarding grain lines are always followed, because the butting of pattern pieces precise with no overlapping and the pattern count is automatic, a boon in complex markers.

It is difficult to compare the capital cost of the computer system used in marker planning with the other methods described previously because in all cases the computer systems provide a pattern development and grading facility as well. It also enables the reproduction of as many copies of a marker as are required without restoring to additional methods of reproduction such as the manual methods required.

After planning the marker on the computer, the marker planner instructs the computer to plot the marker automatically on to paper.

As an alternative to plot in even this amount of information on a marker, it is possible, cutting will be computer-controlled knife, not to plot any of the marker but to attach adhesive labels to the top ply of fabric to give the information necessary to section garment parts into bundles. this saves both the time of plotting and the cost of plotter and paper.

Pressing

PRESSING

Pressing Tool

Pressing makes a large contribution to the finished appearance of garments and thus attractiveness at the point of sale.

THE PURPOSE of pressing

1. To smoothing away unwanted creases and crash marks

In garment manufacture) creases and crashing occur **if** garments as a result of operator handling and these are *particularly* bad where garments/ are handled between operations *in* bundles, when they are tied tightly or piled of trolleys or in boxes.

2. To make creases where the design of the garment requires them

Creases are obvious design features in trousers., skirts (where a series of creases is often referred to as pleating and some collsu sTyles. Creases are less obvious but still require pressing when they are hems and cuff edges, front edges, top edges of waistbands, pocket flaps .edges as well as pressed open seams, which from a pressing *point of view* are two creases seem together.

3. To mould the garment to the contour of the body

it is mainly affected in wool or wool-rich fabrics in the types of garment referred to as tailored. This sort of molding involves two kinds of Reformation (together or separate): shrinking and stretching, the moulding is not possible to unpick the seams and return garment parts to their former fiat state.

4. To prepare garments for further sewing

The term 'under pressing[5] is reserved fox pressing operations on partly constructed garments, while top-of the final pressing *is* used for completed garments, the actual term varying according to the sector of the industry. The stages at which a garment is under pressed will depend en many factors, it normally takes place when several sewing stages hare been completed out are accessible by the press equipment

5. To refinish the fabric after manufacturing the garment

Especially during under pressing, the surface- of the fabric may be temporarily changed. A common symptom is gloss or glazing, induced by extreme pressure of press or ironing order to achieve a firm edge or seam. The surface fibers are heavily flattened in such a. way as to form a partial mirror.

PRESSING EQUIPMENT AND METHODS

In practice, many companies combine the use of several type of pressing equipment to achieve satisfactory audi economical pressing. The following are the different pressing equipments used in garment industry.

- Iron
- Steam Presses
- Steam air finisher
- Steam tunnel
- Pleating
- Permanent press

IRON

The traditional form of iron, heated by a gas flame inside the metal casting, had its last, stronghold in the touching up of men's jackets. Temperature was estimated only by the rate of saliva, evaporation from its bottom surface. A. damp rag provided moisture wand a. piece of linen was the drying agent. The most common type of iron in general use nowadays is steam electric. Tl ic iron is heated by an electric element, controlled by a thermostat, and supplied with steam, either from the factory's main steam supply, or from a small boiler adjacent to the pressing.unit. The steam function of the iron is activated by the touch of a button, when a powerful jet of dry steam is produced. At extremes, the weights of irons vary from, about 2 to 15 kilos. Several shapes are available including a roughly triangular one similar to a domestic iron, the tailor's shape' which has a pointed nose and parallel sides, and a narrow one used for operations such as seam opening on sleeves and trouser legs.

There is a range of workplaces available for ironing, in a situation where a variety of parts and shapes of garments has to be pressed, a Simple pressing table, similar in shape to a domestic ironing board, is used. Modern tables have a supply of vacuum to hold the garment in position and dry and set it alter ironing. This vacuum facility can also be used as work aid in the sense that the term was used earlier. A section of a flat garment neat can be held in place while the operator moves the remainder of the part to create a fold or pleat which she then presses. The position of the fold tan be marked on the press cover for accuracy. The fiat table can be fitted with swivel arms, when present bucks of varied shapes to *allow* the laying of sleeves, shoulders and collars without distortion or the danger of creasing.

Each of these has the vacuum facility. Alternatively, the basic table map consist of a very large flat area, or a smaller curved surface* each with additional sections to be swing into position if required. The *principle* is one of flexibility, with some units able to accept a change of pressing outface so that the most suitable shape is always available for the production of a particular batch of garments. Allowing function is also available on some of these pressing surfaces which gives a billowing surface on which to press. This enables some difficult materials, such as thin, hard rainwear fabrics, to be pressed with less risk of seam impressions showing.

Self contained units, incorporating a steam boiler and electrically driver vacuum and air blowing facilities, are increasingly use both in the under pressing of tailored garments and the pressing of unstructured garments, because they can be moved from place to place at much less cost than conventional steam supply. This means that they can be sued within a production line of sewing operations to enable under pressing to be undertaken at minimum cost.

STEAM PRESSES

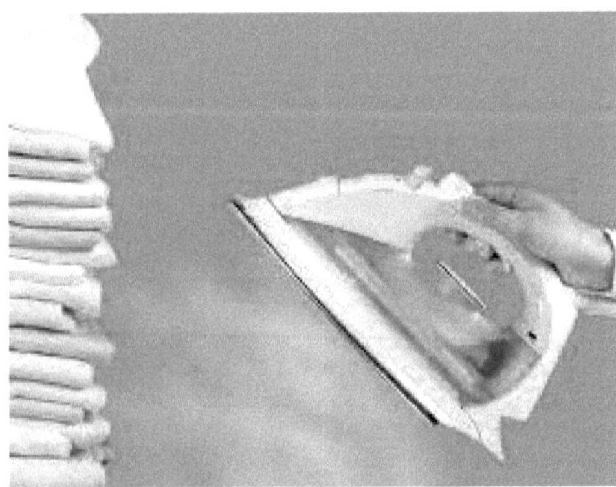

Basic Steam Presser

A steam press consists of a static buck and a head of complementary shape which closes onto it, thus sandwiching the garment to be pressed. A general-purpose, manually carrying the buck, which is generally rounded in shape for pressing a varicty" of garmcnts, linkagcs to closc the head by a scissors action, a pipe system distributing steam to head and buck, a. vacuum system to provide auction through the buck, a table around the buck to aid handling of the garment, end foot controls for head closure and vacuum, with hand and/or foot controls for steam.. There is also a means of varying head pressure, When pressing a garment such as a *skirt,* a typical pressing cycle might be: steam from the buck is applied, the head is locked to press the garment, further steam from the head or the buck may be applied, nod the head is then release, and vacuum applied to cool and dry the garment before it is moved around the buck for the next part of it to be pressed. When pressing is completed, the garment is hung on a hanger. Adequate time of application of vacuum is essential if the garment is not to remain damp and to distort at this stage.In many cases, an iron is available beside the press for the operator 'to touch up local areas of the garment before pressing with the head of the press. This facility can also be used to add sections of fusible interlining to partly constructed garments, especially tailored jackets. Manually operated scissor-action presses have been improved considerably by the use of electronically controlled pneumatic power. The compressed air takes the heavy, fatiguing work of closing the press from the operator, and allows the introduction of automatic timing of the pressing cycle.Another improvement is in the mechanical principle in the operation of steam presses. This employs a vertical head movement instead of a scissors action, giving the benefits of much finer control and a more even distribution of pressure over the whole surface of the buck, especially where contoured shapes have to be aligned. At the same time additional functions can be incorporated such as head vacuum and air blowing from the buck. The combination of these three factors enables easier pressing of fabrics such as gabardines.

CAROUSEL PRESS

A development in press operation is the carousel press. Here a pair of bucks rotates between the operator and either a single or a double head, depending on whether the bucks are identical or .an opposite pair for pressing the left mid right of a garment part. The operator loads the garment onto one buck which is then moved away to be aligned under the bead, often behind a screen that keeps steam away from the operator.

TROUSER PRESSING

Trouser pressing is conventionally carried out in two operations, in addition to the under pressing of the seam; legging on a flat press which sets and creases the legs, and topping in a series of lays around the top of the trouser on a contoured press. If the trouser ‘features a pleat at the waistband, the leg crease must be run into it accurately.

STEAM AIR FINISHER

This equipment is often referred to as a 'puffer‘, a form press or a 'dolly' press, it consists of a frame carrying o steam distribution system, compressed, air distribution system and a pressing from which is a canvas bag in the approximate shape of the garment to *be* pressed that is, a. body shape but with no sleeves. There are controls for steam and air release, arid timers controlling the steam and air cycles. The equipment aims to reduce the positioning and repositioning in pressing operations by pressing the whole garment at the same time, though finishing is a better term in this situation since very little pressure is applied to the garment. The operator pails the garment on to the form from above, and the form is then expanded to its lull size and shape as steam is blown through it: from the inside. A cycle of, perhaps, 3 seconds steaming is followed by a further period of hot air drying, also by blowing from the inside. This equipment can remove accidents‘ creases and refinish the fabric; cur will not form creases or mould the garment. It is extremely useful for garments such as nightdresses, tee shirts and blouses, and is sometimes worth using for simple dresses, even though, the hem might have to be pressed that separated with a iron or a steam press.

STEAMS TUNNEL

Another garment finishing process where pressure is not applies, to me garments but where handling during the process is reduced is in steam tunnel finishing. It can be used for a variety of simple garments in man-made fibers and blends. Some garments would be on hangers, fed under automatic control through a cabinet on a motorized rail, and passing through sections with superheated steam and drying by air blowing. Alternatively, tee shirts and similar knitwear are loaded onto frames and passed through the tunnel on a conveyor. The tunnel reduces the need, for any other pressing process before or after its operation and sometimes eliminates it The arm of the steam is to relax natural fibers, that of the heat to relax man-made fibers. With the garments on hangers or frames, gravity or tension pulls cut the wrinkles, and the turbulence of air blowing provides additional energy to relax wrinkles in woven fabrics. Such turbulence should be restricted with fabrics such, as acrylics, since excessive agitation makes the fabric pliable and subject to deformation. This, fabric responds well to infra-red drying, a feature of some tunnels.

PLEATING

Pleating is a special type of pressing, the aim of which is to produce an array of creases in a garment, of some durability and according to **a** geometrical pattern.. This may be an overall pattern of small pleats, formed as **a** result of machine pleating a complete roll of cloth, or larger pleats formed by basic pleating of garment sections which have been previously cut to snaps and, in the case o: skirt sections, hemmed. Examples of machine pleating are fluting arid crystal pleating and of hand pleating, box pleats **aim** the **tan**-shaped pleats which taper to nothing at the waist and are known as sunray pleats. Like other terms of pressing, the means of pleating **are** heat, moisture and pressure,Machine pleating is of two types. The first is a rotary machine in which the rollers are fitted with complementary dies similar la gears. Second is a blade machine in which pleats are formed by the thrust action of a blade or blades. The pleats are set by heat and pressure as they pass between a pair of mangle-type *Toilers.*

PERMANENT PRESS

The process known as 'permanent press' was developed some years ago as a way of giving good crease recover after washing to cellulose fabrics. It declined with the rise in popularity of polyester / cotton and polyester /viscose blends, where the polyester content assists crease recovery and improves fabric strength". More recently, in an attempt to complete with man-made fibers, the process has been marketed again with 100 percent cotton fabrics of high-enough initial strength to allow for some degradation.

FUSING

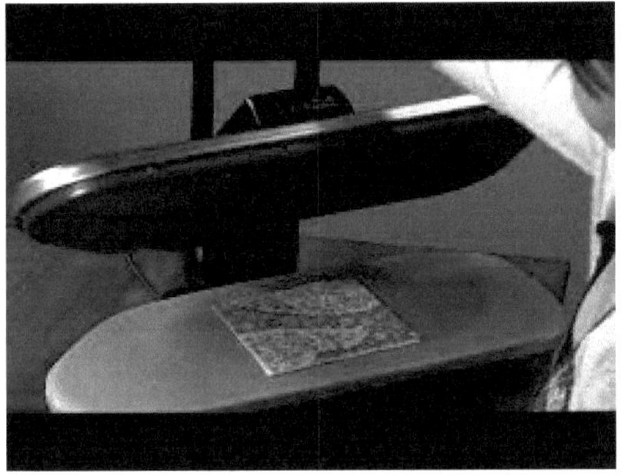

Basic Fusing Machine

Fusing or otherwise known as interfacing gives support and stabilizes areas of a panel ready to be attached to a garment. Interfacing is also used for reinforcing and preventing fabric from stretching. Interfacing works by applying heat which melts the glue and in turn bonds the fusing to the fabric. There are certain areas of sewing where you can put your sewing machine aside and “sew” with a wide range of heat sensitive, iron on sewing aids. Timesaving and easy to use, these fusible's iron-ons and fusible webs are a fundamental part of today's sewing, An iron-on is applied using heat and pressure only, no steam. Mending tape, mending patches and some hem tapes are today's most common iron-ons. However as technology improves, more iron-on products are available. For quick glamour, there are embroidered appliqués and sequin trims that can be applied with the touch of your iron. A fusible is applied using a combination of heat, steam and pressure. Fusible products include interfacings and fusible web. Both fusible and iron-on products come with instructions unless you buy interfacing off a large roll. If your fusing comes with instructions, be sure to follow them carefully. To be on the safe, always use a press cloth to protect your fabric. Fusible web is an adhesive web that glues two layers of fabric together. Don't confuse fusible web with fusible interfacing. Fusible web will not shape, support or reinforce your fabric the way fusible interfacing will. In fact if you examine fusible web carefully, you will see that it is not fabric at all. Its a network of fibres. When the prescribed combination of heat, steam and pressure is applied, these fibres melt and disappear, causing the two layers of fabric to adhere to one another. Use it as a substitute for hand tacking to keep facings etc from rolling to the outside of a garment. Fuse-baste with fusible web. Position the web between the two layers of fabric, cover with a damp press cloth and press lightly for two to three seconds. This basting method is great for preventing ribbons, trims etc from rippling and shifting as they are stitched. Its also a useful technique when sewing lapped seams on fabrics that cannot be pinned, such as synthetic suede. Hems on casual clothes and children's garments can be fused in place instead of sewing. Design your own appliqués and fuse them in place with fusible web. Draw the shape directly on the right side of the fabric. Place the fabric, right side up over the fusible web then cut out both layers at the same time. This is a great way to cover tears and worn spots in children's garments. As general rule by the interfacing that suits the fabric that you are working with so for instance if you are making a jacket and the fabric is a heavy twill, then apply a heavy fusing to match the fabric and on the other hand if you are working with a light fabric, apply a lightweight fusing. If you are working with light interfacing be careful not to have the iron to hot as this will curl and burn the fusing. The best way is to apply

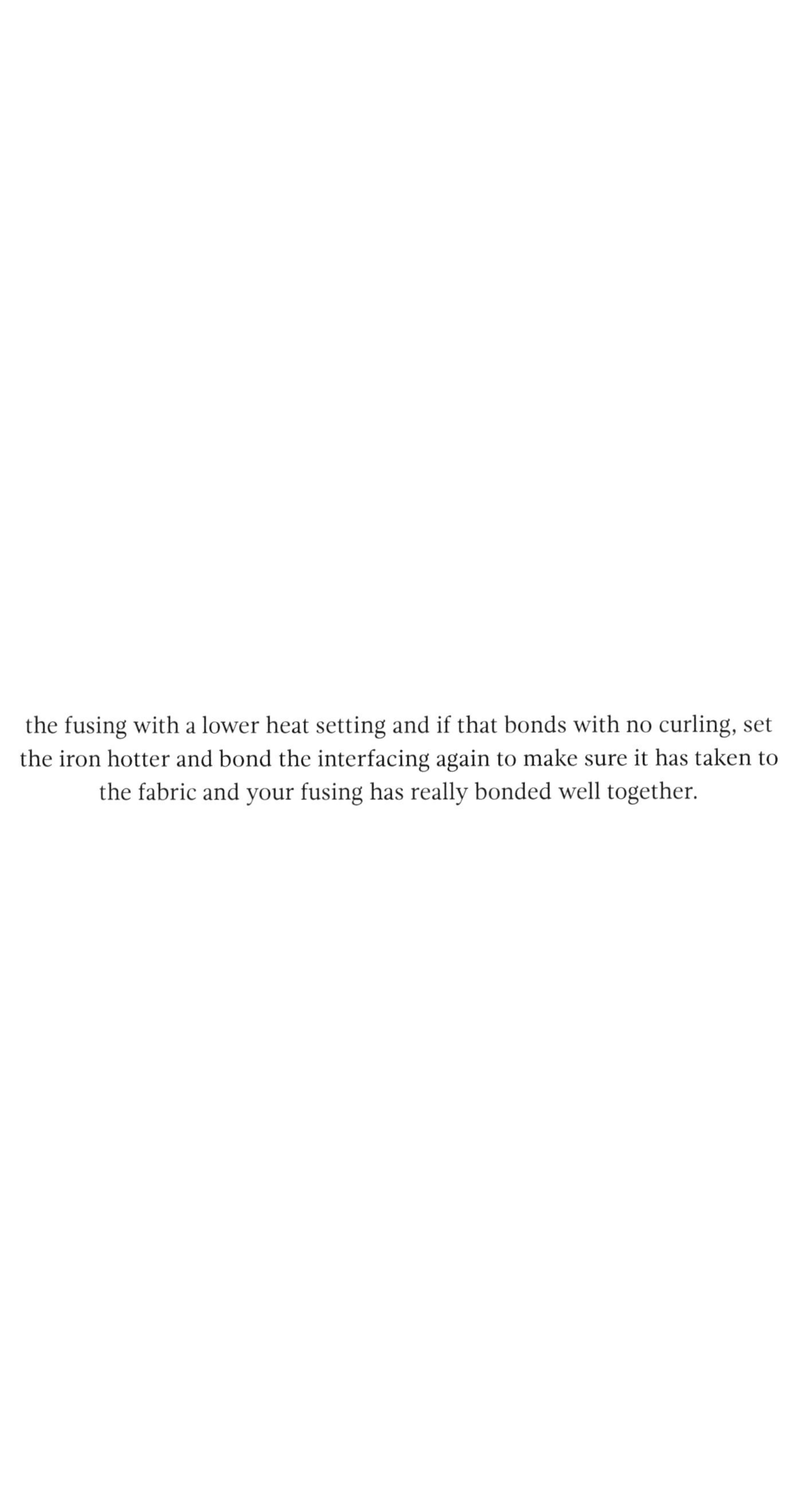

the fusing with a lower heat setting and if that bonds with no curling, set the iron hotter and bond the interfacing again to make sure it has taken to the fabric and your fusing has really bonded well together.

CHAPTER V

Care and Maintainence

CARE AND MAINTENANCE OF SEWING MACHING

Most sewing machine problems that encounter can be traced to poor general maintenance or neglect. But with some simple tools and just a few minutes daily, weekly, or monthly depending on how much our sewing machine, we can help keep our machine running smoothly. Here are my guidelines for care that should keep sewing machine happy and out of the repair shop.

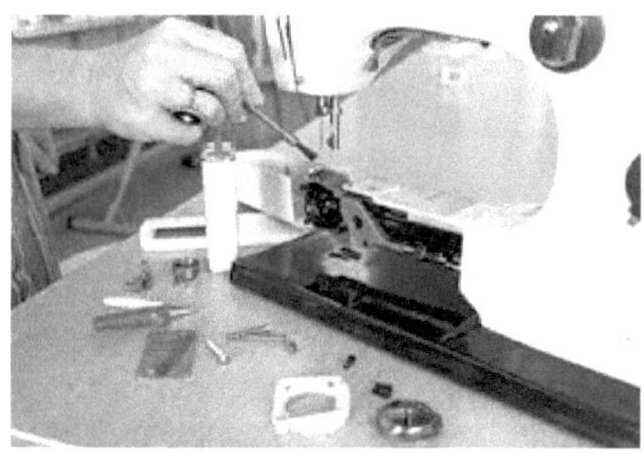

Care and Maintainence of Sewing Machine

- **GENERAL CLEANING**

Cleaning the machine, it is best to clean on e area at a time. Remove only the parts that are involved and be sure to note where each part is from, its position, and which side is top. Remove all the parts possible in order to clean the machine thoroughly. Keep the parts in order to make it easier to place them. When using a screw driver, put the pressure on the push, not on the twist. If a screw will not loosen easily, soak it with cleaning fluid. Then set the screw dirver in the slot and tap sharply with a hammer before attempting to looser. The screw driver blade should be as wide as the slot in the screw is long. Always use a wrench not pliers-on bolt.

First, remove the needle, presser foot, slide plate, throat plate, bobbin case, and the face plate (if it comes off). Put them in the pan and cover with cleaning fluid. Set aside to soak while cleaning other areas.Next, wrap the motor (if necessary) and wire with plastic wrap to protect them from oil and cleaning solvent. Be sure the machine has been unplugged. Now it is time to begin work to clean the machine head. With a sharp pointed tool, clean out all oil holes. Then, with your hand, turn the hand wheel to run the machine. At the same time, squirt cleaning fluid into all the oil holes, on all bearings and on all other places where one part rubs against or turns within another.

- **BOBBIN AREA**

If possible, remove the bobbin case to remove all lint and stray threads. If the machine begins to run hard, it is a sign that dirt or lint has jammed inside a bearing. Continue running the machine and flushing with cleaning fluid until the dirt and gummed oil are washed from the bearing. When the machine runs easily again, tip the head and flush the parts underneath the machine-all oil holes, bearing and places that rub against or within another. Continue running the machine by hand until it functions smoothly.

- **UPPER THREAD TENSION**

Pull a piece of cloth soaked in solvent back and forth between discs to clean. To remove any remaining dirt and oil, dip a cloth or brush in cleaning fluid and scrub all parts of machine that can be reached. Use a needle, knife or other pointed instrument to dig or scrap away any remaining gummed dirt or lint in the feed dog, around the bobbin case, and in other areas.Check the lower tension of the bobbin case and the upper thread tension discs. Pull a thread under the tension of the bobbin to remove dirt. Pull a piece of cloth soaked in cleaning fluid back and forth between the discs of the upper tension. Repeat with a dry cloth to be sure no lint or thread is caught between them.In addition to general cleaning, three areas need special attention. They include the hand wheel bearing and the clutch assembly, the needle-bar and the presser foot, and the hook and bobbin areas assembly. When the hand wheel assembly gets gummed and dirty, it must be cleaned for the clutch to work properly. The clutch disengages the needle-bar when winding a bobbin.Some new sewing machines refill the bobbin in its regular position and a clutch is not necessary. In such machines, it is not often necessary to remove the hand wheel to clean this area.

- **HAND WHEEL AREA**

To remove the clutch and hand wheel, loosen the small screw in the face of the locknut (the locknut is the part that is turned to the left to release the clutch for operation the bobbin winder). Next, unscrew the locknut, and remove the washer and hand wheel. Most machines will have a washer that looks like one of the three shown. Some makes will be slightly different. Notice the position of the washer so it can put in back in the same position.Clean the hand wheel, washer, and shaft. Lubricate the shaft with two drops of oil and place a small amount of grease on all gears. Reassemble the hand wheel and clutch. If the clutch fails to operate, either because it will not hold or fails to release, remove the locknut again and turn the washer one half turn (180 degree) and reassemble. The clutch should then work properly.After thoroughly cleaning these areas, reassemble the machine and run it by hand. It should run smoothly if all parts have been replaced correctly.

- **FACE PLATE AREA**

The face plate on most machines is held in place with one or two screws. By removing these plates can be easily removed for cleaning of the needle-bar and presser foot bar.On some of the newer machines, the face plate is a part of a housing that is mounted on hinges, which makes it easy to move the entire housing away from the bars and mechanisms behind it. Not other parts need to be removed for cleaning in this area. First use a dry brush to clean out all lint and other foreign material. A small piece of cloth with a little solvent on it can be used to clean the needle-bar and presser bar of any gummy grease.After thoroughly cleaning, place a drop or two of oil on each shaft where it slides through the housing. Oil all other moving parts according to instruction book before replacing face plate.

- **BOBBIN AND HOOK AREA**

Lint is the primary offender in this area. The bobbin case can be removed on all makes of machines. Use a dry brush to clean out all lint. Remove any thread that may be wound up around for more complete cleaning. Place one drop of oil on the exterior perimeter of the hook and the bobbin race to lubricate if after cleaning.

- **OILING AND LUBRICATING THE MACHINE**

Allow the machine to stand overnight so excess cleaning fluid can evaporate before oiling and lubricating it. Check the machine instruction booklet to determine the type of oil lubricant to use and where to use them.Some machines have bearings that are nylon or graphite-impregnated bronze and do not require oil or lubricant. Also, some machines do not need oiling because they are designed with oil impregnated in the bearing castings. If the machine does not require oil, do not use it.Do not oil the tension discs, the hand wheel release or the belts and rubber rings on any machine.In the holes designated, and on all parts that rub against or within another, squirt a little oil. Run the machine by hand to distribute the oil into all the bearings. Use oil freely because all oil has been removed in the cleaning process. If there is any wool or felt pads that feed oil to parts, be sure they are will-oiled.For later oiling, one drop of oil on each bearing and in each oil hole is enough. It is a good practice to oil the machine after each day's work or after 8 to 10 hours of use. Even if do not use the machine often, oil it occasionally to keep the oil from drying and gumming.If the machine requires a lubricant, lubricate the areas suggested. Use the lubricant recommended for the machine for best results.After oiling and lubrication the machine, wipe away excess oil and reassemble the machine. As replace the parts that have been soaking in the pan, do not force screws or parts into place. Check to be sure it is in the correct location.

CHAPTER VI

Latest Innovation

Latest Sewing Machine Technology That's Making Life Easier (2021)

Since the invention of the sewing machine, various improvements have been made to make the working process more convenient. With the passage of time, different technologies have been implemented in the industry for better productivity. It's necessary for the advancement of society and making an effort put by workers more valuable. In this article, I am going to discuss some of the advanced technologies used in sewing machines. If you don't know, there are primarily three types of sewing machine mechanical, electronics, and computerized; where electronic models are in trend as its simple to use and reduce the effort put by workers whereas the computerized machines are more advanced ones that are used by professional industries for highest precision and accuracy.

Pedal less sewing

During the work on parts that are complex and critical, a lot of time is needed by the operators of the machine to get control at the foot pedals. Moreover, it is difficult for an injured or disabled person to use foot pedals.

So, with the advancement in technologies, various providers offer sewing paddle less version. The advantage of using these is that stitching can be done at a constant speed.

You do not need to move your hands and feet at the same time.

Your foot need not be kept on the machine all the time, you can move them freely. You can also stitch while you are standing.

Changing settings using the android phone

Continuous adjustments are to be made on the settings, based on the garment style used by the operator. If the settings are changed manually in each of the machines, a lot of time will be required. It's the feature that you'll not find in every machine, but it should be there in smart ones.

Voice guide in sewing machines

A breakdown can occur. When an issue happens, the line supervisor is to be informed by the operator, and then the supervisor informs the mechanic for solving the problem. As suggested by BestBuyReview, in many cases, the operator is not aware of the potential reason for the breakdown. Voice guide can give notification to the operator about malfunctions of a machine like leakage of oil or break down.

Sewing machines with USB port

Copy of the settings like the length of stitch and stitching speed can easily be done from one unit to the other with the help of a USB port. This USB port can also be used for charging phones or other purposes.

Real-time monitoring

Monitoring the sewing machines by mobiles or tablets can be done easily in any part of the world by linking all those to a server. With this network, the production line status can be monitored in real-time. Moreover, any malfunctions which may happen in the course of production can be detected

Vision Sewing

Vision sewing is one of the best features found in some advanced models. With this option, stitches can be made easily. In vision sewing, objects and fabric need to be placed on the machine; a photo of the setup is taken by the camera.The area of the applied item is defined by the system by analyzing the picture, and a stitch pattern is generated automatically. Vision sewing does not require almost any skill of the operator, and everything is done much faster. This way series of numbers or letters can be sewed in a single move.

Modular Machines

The modular sewing machine has room to change and fit components for adjusting to the requirements of the future. This made the models flexible, eliminating the requirement of buying new models when the demand for fitting in new components arises.

Digital Feed System

An increase in productivity is an important factor in this industry. With this increase in production, labor costs are also increased. So due to this rise in costs, advanced models are needed. For the improvement in productivity and reduction of labor costs, digital feed systemin sewing machines plays an essential role.

Printed by Libri Plureos GmbH in Hamburg,
Germany